CHRIST'S
HOSPITAL

First published 1984

ISBN 086364 005 2

© Town & County Books 1984

Published by Ian Allan Ltd, Shepperton, Surrey;
and printed by Ian Allan Printing Ltd at their works
at Coombelands in Runnymede, England.

Contents

For Angus Ross

*Scholar, Donation Governor and Chairman
of the Council of Almoners*

The Worshipful the Treasurer of Christ's Hospital

Preface

The late George Allan was a boy at Christ's Hospital from 1897 to 1902, the seismic years which saw preparations for the move of the Boys' School from its ancient home in Newgate Street to Sussex. For most of his adult life he served the Foundation, from 1933 to 1946 as Clerk.

The book was first published in 1937 and appeared again, as revised by George Allan himself, ten years later.

It was at the invitation of the original author's son Ian, himself an Almoner of Christ's Hospital, that I undertook the preparation of this new, and necessarily much-amended, edition. This invitation I accepted with much reluctance for there must be some suspicion of impertinence in tampering with the work of a man, as was George Allan, deeply immersed in the history and administration of the Foundation and, as was George Allan, unshakeably committed to the perpetuation of its spirit of charity. But, onerous as it has been in some respects, the task has also been a delight for in its performance I am able to repay some small part of the great debt which I owe to Christ's Hospital.

Such difficulties as there have been have been eased – and my pleasure enhanced – because, as always is the case in Christ's Hospital affairs, my pleas for assistance have been answered eagerly and efficiently.

David Young, of the Christ's Hospital Office, prepared the index; for that both the publisher and I owe him gratitude; but my thanks go to him also for his enthusiastic and scholarly assistance in resolving several historical conundrum.

Many of the illustrations in this volume are evidence to Alan Hollingsworth's skill as a photographer.

It is a rare and amiable feature of the Christ's Hospital community that so often the wives of Old Blues take to themselves voluntarily the loyalty and affection for the Foundation that their husbands owe out of duty and gratitude. My wife, herself a Donation Governor, has assisted me with much more than moral support in the preparation of all my books but I suspect that never before has she felt such deep involvement as has been hers whilst I have been working on this volume.

Another Old Blue wife, my dear friend, Elaine Barr, has helped me in various ways. To her and to her colleague at the Victoria and Albert Museum, Michael Snodin, my thanks are particularly due for notably expert advice about the silver which forms such a handsome part of C.H. treasures.

The dedication to Angus Ross is no mere dutiful formality. His wisdom and care as Christ's Hospital approaches the second metamorphosis of this century, the re-unification of its two Schools, must secure for him a place among the greatest of all Treasurers but I honour him also for many decades of friendship and – to me more surprising – for the fact that he read part of the typescript without battering with me so much as one of his customary caustic comments.

My thanks go also to my secretary, Deborah Brown. After typing and re-typing from the manuscript she must now know as much as do I about the Foundation, and almost as much as did George Allan. I owe much to her accuracy and more to her unshakeable good humour.

J. E. Morpurgo
Scholar, Donation Governor
and Almoner of Christ's Hospital

The

Religious, Royal, and Ancient Foundation

of

CHRIST'S HOSPITAL

May those prosper who love it,

and

may God increase their number

CHAPTER ONE

Origin and Growth

Christ's Hospital boasts a literature richer than that of any other school. It could be no more than happy coincidence but, more likely, it has been the unique traditions of the Hospital and their profound sense of community and of gratitude to the Foundation which, over the centuries, have persuaded Blues in all generations to set to print their tributes and their recollections of school-days in poem, essay and book. Certainly – and this too may be either accident or inherited respect for the literary arts – Christ's Hospital has been unusual among schools in the number of its sons who have made their adult careers in literature or in journalism or who, though passing their lives in some other calling, have shown nevertheless by occasional exercise a rare gift as writers. Of these, the professionals and the skilled amateurs, almost every one has at some time saluted Christ's Hospital.

In this plush literary record the glorious conjunction of Coleridge, Lamb and Leigh Hunt – three who stand close to the summit of English literary achievement – has enshrined the ethos of the Hospital forever firm in the minds of readers far outside the intimate circle, but they had their noble precursors – George Peele and David Baker among them – their articulate contemporaries – W. P. Scargill, T. S. Surr and the first great editor of *The Times*, Thomas Barnes – and they have had a host of brilliant successors. In this century, for example, Edmund Blunden, one of England's finest writers, devoted a whole book to Christ's Hospital and supplemented it with several poems, with essays and with a myriad of allusions. Middleton Murry, Philip Youngman Carter, Graham Hutton, Sydney Carter, Michael Swan, Keith Douglas, Percy Young, Barnes Wallis (seemingly from a world quite other than the literary but in this patently a man of letters) and (in a brave attempt to bowl on an unfamiliar wicket) the England cricketer, John Snow: all have written on Christ's Hospital.

This outpouring of praise, reminiscence and explanation has been so various and so continuous that, in 1953, it was possible to put together, exclusively from the writings of those who had been educated in the school or who had served the Foundation, a representation of the four hundred years of Christ's Hospital history and of the panoply of its traditions. Such too is the world-wide interest in the mysteries of this unique institution that *The Christ's Hospital Book* was bought everywhere, even in the United States, Canada, Australia and New Zealand, and was, by the crudest commercial measure, successful as no other similar act of piety.

There have been also many formal histories but of these most were too detailed, too obviously written for those who understood already the eccentric nature of the Hospital – and many too turgid – to arouse much attention from a public outside the ever-interested parochial audience.

It was with the intention of explaining to this larger constituency the idiosyncratic purposes, the peculiar organisation and the especial characteristics of Christ's Hospital that the late G. A. T. Allan, himself a devoted Blue and the much-loved and much-respected Clerk of Christ's Hospital, prepared the first version of this book for publication in 1937.

George Allan was commissioned to write his book as one in a series on the Great Public Schools of Britain. Set in that context the invitation was an anomaly, a blatant demonstration of a contradiction which must be resolved from the outset if the true nature of the Foundation is to be understood. Except by the meanest and most legalistic definition – by the presence of the Head Master of the Boys' School as a member of the Headmasters' Conference – Christ's Hospital is not a public school at all, as generally the world understands that term. Indeed, the principles upon which the school was established and has been continued for almost four-and-a-half centuries are close to being antithetical to those which prevail in most public schools.

Christ's Hospital is an independent school, and jealous of its independence, but it is, first and above else, a charity.

So also, it may be argued, were many of the great public schools in their origins and so also are they all to this day by the nice (and convenient) measure of legal status. But Christ's Hospital stands virtually alone in that it has remained true to the charitable intentions of its sixteenth century Founders and alone in that its charitable purposes transcend all others. More even than that: by the oldest and most generous interpretation of the word, Christ's Hospital is the quintessential charity, the product of a 'dede of pittie', the continuing consequence of acts of love. The words of the Schools Inquiry Commissioners ring as true to-day as they did when first they were written in 1867:

Christ's Hospital is a thing without parallel in this country, and *sui generis*. It is a grand relic of the medieval spirit – a monument of the profuse munificence of that spirit, and of that constant stream of individual beneficence which is so often found to flow around institutions of that character.

We have always been a school for both boys and girls. The Christ's Hospital Girls' School is, in fact, the oldest school for girls in the country ('a poor young maiden child' is recorded in the earliest extant record of admissions – for 9th December, 1554 – and another girl is, if only by the accident of the alphabet, the first whose name appears in the Registers, unbroken since 1563). But there are many public schools for girls and now many public schools that are co-educational, as soon we will be also, and it is not this concession to equal opportunities for the sexes which sets Christ's Hospital apart from the public schools. The fundamental, and patently charitable, distinction is evidenced most surely by contrasting the principles which control the Hospital's conditions for the admission of children with those which influence the governing bodies of the public schools at large.

With only limited exceptions parents who look to educate their children in a public school must first 'enter' them – register them as candidates – and then, once the child has passed the appropriate examination, that child is enrolled, *providing always that the parents can pay the required fees.*

Christ's Hospital works in contrary fashion. The first and, for most prospective Blues, the all-important stipulation is "that no child will be admitted whose parents or next friends are not, in the opinion of the Council of Almoners, in need of assistance towards his education and maintenance."

From this over-riding consideration there stems a consequence which creates another and no less significant difference between the community at large which is Christ's Hospital and the communities – children and former pupils – of the public schools. As 'need' is the prime criterion a parent must meet before entering his child as a Scholar of Christ's Hospital (and in this usage, too, the Hospital is unique: all its children are 'scholars', at least by the courtesy of

nomenclature) so also, by definition, are those parents unable to offer to their children the benefits of financial support, family influence or powerful contacts to help them on their way after they leave school. It has therefore been imperative upon the Hospital that, if it is to carry out to the full its charitable purposes, it must continue the care of its children even after they complete their formal education.

This part of its self-imposed responsibility it has fulfilled faithfully from the sixteenth century until to-day but the fraternity (what one irreverent member of the community has called 'the Old Blue Mafia') has always shown itself to be an effective substitute for family patronage.

In all it is the manner in which Christ's Hospital's men and women have consistently overcome the initial handicap of poverty and the inhibition of lack of influence – the phenomenally high "success-rate" – which, in an age dedicated to equal opportunity for all, makes Christ's Hospital precepts and methods much more than merely fascinating. The Hospital must be a model, to be imitated, cherished – and never to be destroyed.

There is one more characteristic which demands attention even thus early in the narrative, a characteristic which differentiates if from the public schools, and which re-inforces the boast that it is, above all else, a charity and the active heir to the noblest of charitable instincts. For more than three hundred years parents gave nothing towards the costs of education and maintenance and even in this century their contribution has been minimal. Therefore the Hospital has depended for its financial stability entirely on generous benefactors. Happily, there have been many such and among their number a goodly proportion have been sons and daughters of the House. In a manner that is almost a miraculous justification of the School's Christian ethos and proof that it is, in every sense, a charity, Christ's Hospital has been throughout its history largely self-perpetuating. The response to Appeals launched since the Second World War has demonstrated that it is not only Blues who have prospered who have answered the call to make some financial recompense for the benefits received in youth for, to-day as in the past, the weight of this duty must fall upon those who can bear it and these are the very men and women who are debarred from entering their own children into the Hospital. They have never failed to carry this burden and there can be no other school in the world which educates the children of other men and women at the expense of those who, by their own skills and exertions, have worked themselves out of the possibility that they can confer upon their own offspring the privileges which they themselves enjoyed in youth.

Henry VIII wrought better than he intended when he took from the Grey Friars their properties close to St. Paul's Cathedral and bestowed them on the City of London "for the relief of the poor". For six years this gift lay dormant. Then it was that Bishop Ridley's strident sermon on Charity moved the heart of Henry's young son and stirred Edward VI to seek further and more practical advice from Ridley. King, Bishop, the Lord Mayor and Aldermen conferred and, in 1552, settled for the establishment of three Royal Hospitals: Christ's (in the Grey Friars), for the education of poor children; St. Thomas's, for the care of the sick; and Bridewell, for the correction of "the idle and vagabonds".

The learned writer of the 1837 "Report of the Commissioners for Inquiring concerning Charities" says, in his own inimitable style, that

it was not a refounding or extension of any charitable foundation of a similar nature already endowed and existing on the same spot previously to the dissolution of the monasteries, but a new foundation owing its commencement to the active benevolence of some distinguished citizens of London, stimulated perhaps in the first instance by the extreme distress to which the suppression of the religious houses had reduced many of the mendicant poor, but eventually directed into a more beneficial channel than that of mere eleemosynary distribution.

The earliest history of the Foundation is contained in a precious manuscript, the work of John Howes, citizen, grocer and at one-time apprentice and servant to our first Treasurer, Richard Grafton, whose printing-press produced (within the Hospital's precincts) his own edition of the Bible. Howes became Renter of the Hospital (collector of rents) and as such it was one of his duties to attend upon the scrutineers of the Hospitals, for they had at first a common chest, and to "inquire and search out for all the legacies so given, and make thereof rehearsal to the scrutineers or gatherers of them, who shall receive the same". Howes was paid on commission: "He shall have of every £ received two pence and none other fee or wages."

The Howes manuscript is in the form of "a familiar and friendly discourse dialoguewise setting forth the first order and manner of the erection of the Hospitals of Christ, Bridewell and St. Thomas the Apostle". Bound in white vellum, mystic, wonderful, the document was produced in the Court of Chancery a century later and duly endorsed as an exhibit. Like the Ark of the Covenant it then disappeared from history; but unlike the Ark it was re-discovered after two hundred years amongst the lumber of a disused store-room.

See how the good seed germinated. A committee of thirty was appointed which did commonly meet every day in the inner chamber of the Guildhall. In counting the cost of their undertaking they first thought good to begin with themselves, and each gave his contribution of £10 or £20 according to his ability. Then they exhorted the preachers, ministers, churchwardens and sidesmen to obtain from their parishioners a frank benevolence and weekly pension. And to that effect they delivered therewith a very fine, witty, and learned oration, being printed, which they gave to every preacher and minister, the better to instruct and persuade the people in every parish to give liberally.

The Annual Accounts for 1552 – and we possess still an unbroken series of accounts from that day to this – show that this witty oration, added perhaps to the solicitations of interested friends, was not without tangible result. The heading of the first page runs as follows:

A perfect and full declaration of all such sums of money as have been from time to time given not only of the free and liveral disposition of divers Aldermen and Commoners, Governors of this House, and of the several gifts of other, but also received by a monthly collection throughout the Wards of the City of London towards the relief and sustentation of the poor of Christ's and St. Thomas's Hospitals and the members and parts thereof as hereafter more plainly shall appear.

And, having run for two years, the account ends:

Summa totalis of all the charge of Christ's Hospital sythen the time of the erection thereof unto the last day of the month of June anno 1554 as well as in building beds and other furniture as may particularly appear by the account amounteth £4641, 6s. 9d.

Civic benevolence was thus the first stone in our structure. After the spontaneous contributions of the Committee of Thirty came an application to the Aldermen, then to the City Companies, whose subscriptions are set out in detail by Howes. The first gift in kind came from one of the thirty, who took upon himself to provide 500 feather beds, 500 pads of straw to lay under them, as many blankets, and a thousand pair of sheets. The King, acceding to the suppliant Ridley, gave his palace of Bridewell, a truly royal gift – on paper. But Howes says naively that "it was not without an infinite charge, and the situation thereof was such that all the cost was cast away, there was no coming to it but through sinking lanes or over a filthy ditch which did so continually annoy the house that the King had no pleasure in it". Edward also handed over the Savoy and its lands. The account includes money received from the sale of such articles as "one dozen of silver spoons weighing 34 oz. at 4s 8d. the oz., £7, 18s 8d.". By royal warrant, all the linen belonging to the churches in London – save only sufficient for their own needs – was brought to the Governors for the use of the poor, this being of especial service to St. Thomas's.

The City itself was not slow to do its share in meeting the increasing expenditure of its healthily-growing nursling. The Common Council in 1548 had granted to St. Bartholomew's Hospital 500 marks out of the profits of Blackwell Hall, the common market-place for woollen and linen goods. In 1557 the profits surplus to these 500 marks were "wholly bestowed to the relief and support of the poor sick and indigent persons in the Hospitals of Christ and St. Thomas for evermore and to no other use". The Hospital eventually became the managers of Blackwell Hall, and as such had to concern itself with discoveries such as are recorded in the following minute: "By the report of Edward Towney, a cardmaker dwelling in Southwark, at a town in Yorkshire called Osset beside Wakefield the best cardwire to make cards is there made, and is to be bought for 9s 0d. the stone after 12 lb. to the stone at the hands of one John Robinson. . . and for the wire made in Gloucestershire one Hill of Gloucester hath the trade of it."

In 1582 the Corporation, which had exercised an immemorial jurisdiction over all persons working carts within the liberties of the City, transferred authority to Christ's Hospital. A carroom (the right to have a cart marked by the Governors) brought the Hospital an annual rent of 17s. 4d., with an entrance fee of twenty shillings. Carts were brought to the Hospital each July for branding, except during those periods when the Woodmongers Company enjoyed the privilege in exchange for an annuity of £150.

As early as 1577 the Governors appear to have evolved another scheme for supplementing income. Persons who desired to be buried with some pomp and circumstance might, from this date and for nearly two hundred years, hire a number of boys and girls to attend and sing at their funerals or to act as mutes. The larger the donation, the more the attendants; and the matter might be arranged by legacy, though the Governors would almost certainly have found some means to insure against an obvious risk.

Gifts of money, houses and lands were quickly and liberally bestowed by those who saw the good work that was being done by the Hospital, and who had an opportunity of noting the intense interest taken by the Governors in their charges and the conscientiousness with which they fulfilled their trust. So impressive was the high standard of integrity displayed by the Governors that a great many persons appointed them trustees corporately, not always with a *quid pro quo* for the Hospital. Many of these sixteenth century trusts are even to-day carried out, to the letter, by the Foundation.

So much for the beginning of the endowments, which continued to increase.

What of the children? Most were taken in for shelter, either from the streets or from homes that were no homes at all. The street-keepers and the beadles were constantly engaged in rounding up those who, without their services must have become in time idlers, vagrants – or worse. There was in those early days no age-limit; during the first twenty years the Hospital opened its charity to babies one day old and to men and women of "forty years and upwards". Some few of the children were foundlings but there was no basket outside the Hospital's gates such as later Captain Coram set before his and, indeed, the most diligent search was made for the parents of children abandoned in the streets – and woe betide them if they were found, as may be seen from this minute:

Wednesday being Embring Day and the 16th December, 1556. Where by the Lord Mayor and his brethren the Aldermen it was adjudged that a woman named Norton dwelling in Southwark for leaving and forsaking of a child in the streets should be whipped at Bridewell and from there sent unto the Governors of Christ's Hospital for a further reformation, which thing being done she was sent unto the pillory in Cheap with a paper on her head wherein was written in great letters Whipped at Bridewell for leaving and forsaking her child in the streets and from thence carried into Southwark and banished for her offence out of the city.

Yet that the Foundation was an educational establishment from the beginning is clearly proven. This is no mere personal opinion, but the mature decision of the Judicial Committee of the Privy Council, which in a judgment delivered in 1889, found that, almost immediately after the foundation, the original site and the large gifts made to it had been applied to education, and that Christ's Hospital's Governing Body, acting separately from 1557 onwards, had been concerned with educational funds. To this conclusion they were drawn above all by the words of the King's indenture of 1553, where the Royal Founder insisted that he graciously considered:

the good and godly endeavours of his most humble and obedient subjects the mayor and commonalty and citizens of London, who diligently by all ways and means do travail for the good provision of the said poor and every sort of them, and that by such sort and means as neither the child in his infancy shall want virtuous education and bringing up, neither when the same shall grow into full age shall lack matter whereon the same may virtuously occupy himself in good occupation or science profitable to the commonweal.

Such was the quality of the education provided in the Hospital that some, even from the first generation of Blues, were sufficiently learned to make their way to Oxford or to Cambridge and many had been so well-trained that they could pass out of school into service as clerks and scriveners.

Many did not remain for long humble servants to the great. A little more than a century after the foundation Daniel Defoe wrote:

Soon the excellent reputation enjoyed by boys reared in Christ's Hospital attracted attention far outside the boundaries of the City of London. In 1616, the Court of Common Council appointed two Deputies to go to Ireland to report on the progress of the plantations in Londonderry and Coleraine. They were "to have special care that those children which were lately sent over for servants and apprentices out of the Hospitals in London, to be employed in both the towns may be well bestowed and placed with honest tradesmen and housekeepers for their better breeding". The Deputies reported in due course that "the twelve children sent over from Christ's Hospital arrived all safe and well at Londonderry and are placed ten of them there and two of them at Coleraine, and these indentures we will deliver to the Treasurer of Christ's Hospital, to be there kept for their use."

This pioneering venture was commemorated by a stained-glass window in Londonderry's Guildhall, with, in one light, a group of boys in their familiar blue-coats and, in another, the Hospital's arms.

Further afield even than Ireland: already almost a decade before the Pilgrim Fathers set foot on Plymouth Rock (and thereby set in train the fallacy, which still persists in popular fable, that they were the creators of the first permanent British settlement in North America) the first Blue had arrived in the well-established Virginia Colony.

The proficiency shown by Thomas Sexton and his many seventeenth and eighteenth century successors so impressed the leading planters of Virginia that the custom of sending "back to the Hospital for a boy who can read well, write clearly and cast accounts" persisted until well after the United States had become an independent nation and, because there too many of these boys stayed on and prospered after their indentures were completed, many prominent families in the Southern States – but particularly in Virginia – can claim a Blue as founding-father.

During the seventeenth century – after the streets had been fairly well cleared and the "City was now in its beauty" – the Governors were much occupied with the age of admission of children and the type of child to be taken in. One of the earliest regulations is to confine admissions to the City.

No foreigner's child, born without the liberties of this City, nor any others, though their parents be free of this City, being born without the said liberties, shall be admitted children of this House, except it be upon very great consideration.

In 1664: "no child under the age of 4 years shall be admitted from any great Personage by letter or otherwise except the same be the child of a freeman of London and born within the said city". Fifteen years later: "no child shall be admitted into this House at the suit of any parish or person whatsoever, except it be of the age of 3 years or more". In 1652 it was ordered that no children be taken in but "such as be freemen's children", and shortly afterwards those were barred who were "lame or otherwise infirm in the body".

By 1676 these various regulations had crystallized. Candidates for admission must be children of freemen, living within the City, not under seven years of age, orphans wanting either father or mother or both; none to be taken in that are foundlings, that have any probable means of being provided for in other ways, "or that are lame, crooked, or deformed, or that have any infectious disease, as the leprosy, scald head, itch, scab, or that have the evil or rupture". Nor might any child be admitted whose brother or sister had already entered.

The progress of the Hospital in its first century was not without hindrances. The Founder King lived but a short time after he set his signature to the Charter, and his sister, Queen Mary I, looked with devout Catholic disfavour upon an institution which made emphatic its essentially Protestant origins by its continued occupation of the Grey Friars. It was her inclination to put an end to this heretical impertinence, but she was engrossed with other burning issues – close to Christs's Hospital in Smithfield – and the Foundation was protected by the affection of the citizens of London.

There survives from the Marian interlude one story which deserves to be authentic. The Founder King, it is said, had conferred upon the Hospital the right to greet the Monarch on the occasion of his first visit to the City. (The origins may be legendary but the privilege undoubtedly exists – and is still exercised.) Queen Mary showed her disdain for the Hospital by turning her back on the boy chosen to present to her its Loyal Address. That boy, so runs the tale, was St. Edmund Campion!

Divine retribution and divine intercession, perhaps, but more likely the Accession of sturdy and Protestant Queen Elizabeth I, saved the Hospital and in her reign it continued to grow and to develop its functions as a school. But growth brought with it new difficulties. The care, spiritual, physical and educational, of so many children created financial anxiety – a burden from which the Governors have seldom been freed. Expenses soared and many City parishes failed to pay their due subscriptions. The Governors borrowed: £1500 from the City Companies and £500 from the Corporation. Even this was not enough and so the Common Council decreed that all fines and forfeitures incurred by Billingsgate porters be made over to the Hospital. (It is not stated if the forfeitures could be paid in kind!) Further, the Common Council called upon the Master and Wardens of the Woodmongers "to shew

Cyttie the Aldermen of

every Companye broug

every of the sortes of th

Dignitie.

Dutie.

It is not to be doubte

The nomber was grea

Of ffatherles childr∢

Of Sore & sicke ps∢

Of poore men over▌

Of aged persons   -

Of decayed househ∢

Of ydell vagabonde▌

The whole nomber

all sortes wch requ

A page from John Howes MS, 1582.

14